Original title:

Shimmering Ice

Author: Mirell Mesipuu

ISBN HARDBACK: 978-9916-79-900-0

ISBN PAPERBACK: 978-9916-79-901-7

ISBN EBOOK: 978-9916-79-902-4

Frozen Reflections

In silence deep, the shadows creep,
Mirrors of ice, where secrets sleep.
Each breath a cloud, each step a grace,
Time stands still in this sacred space.

Crystal blooms in winter's breath,
Whispers of life, yet still in death.
A world transformed, both near and far,
Glimmers of hope beneath the star.

Ethereal Glare

A hint of light in twilight's veil,
Gentle whispers, a soft tale.
Shadows shift in velvet air,
Lost in dreams, without a care.

Glistening stars, a cosmic dance,
Moments fleeting, a timeless chance.
The universe, a canvas wide,
Where secrets of light and fate abide.

Prismatic Chill

Colors burst in the frosty morn,
Nature wakes, a canvas reborn.
Each hue a note in winter's song,
Harmony's call, where we belong.

Eyes behold the vibrant glow,
A fleeting moment, pure as snow.
Fractals form in glacial air,
Echoes of beauty, beyond compare.

Glinting Frost

A dance of light on icy streams,
Nature's crown, spun from our dreams.
Step by step, the world aglow,
A shimmering path where memories flow.

Frosted petals, delicate lace,
Each moment captured, a quiet grace.
In the chill of dawn's embrace,
We find our hearts in this magical place.

Twinkling Crystal Dreams

Stars whisper secrets in the night,
Glistening softly, pure delight.
Each twinkle holds a tale untold,
In crystal dreams, our hopes unfold.

Moonbeams dance on velvet skies,
Painting shadows, silent sighs.
In the stillness, dreams take flight,
Twinkling jewels, a wondrous sight.

Frost-kissed Twilight

As daylight fades to gentle gray,
A frosty breath begins to play.
Whispers of winter paint the trees,
In twilight's glow, a chilling breeze.

Stars begin to pierce the gloom,
Cloaked in silence, dreams assume.
Frost-kissed petals, silver-bound,
In twilight's arms, solace is found.

Ethereal Shard

A shard of light breaks through the haze,
Illuminating forgotten ways.
Within its glow, the world anew,
An ethereal dance in crystal blue.

Whispers float on the evening air,
Carried gently without a care.
In this moment, time stands still,
An ethereal shard, a heart to fill.

Lattice of Light

Threads of gold weave through the dark,
Creating patterns, a radiant spark.
In every corner, shadows play,
A lattice of light at close of day.

Softly glowing, the world unwinds,
Embraced by warmth, solace finds.
In each lattice, dreams entwine,
Illuminated, our souls align.

An Auroral Fracture

In the silent night sky,
Colors swirl and dance bright,
A fracture of pure light,
Whispers of the high fly.

Beneath the cosmic glow,
Dreams awaken and swell,
Nature's breath, a soft swell,
In harmony, we flow.

With each shimmering wave,
Time stands still in wonder,
As night whispers a thunder,
A celestial, bold crave.

Stars blink in reply,
Painting tales of old fate,
While shadows dissipate,
As the dawn draws nigh.

Hold this moment dear,
An aurora's soft grace,
In the stillness, we trace,
A beauty, crystal clear.

Prismatic Winter Breath

Winter casts its soft spell,
With whispers of frost air,
Each breath a crystal flare,
Nature's tale weaves quite well.

Colors shift in the light,
Icicles gleam like bright stars,
Reflecting dreams from afar,
A magical, pure sight.

With every step we take,
Snowflakes dance like fine lace,
Framing our smiling face,
In this world we awake.

The breath of winter's chill,
Wraps us in frosted might,
As day turns into night,
Time moves slow, yet so still.

In the hush of this place,
We find warmth in the cold,
Stories of warmth retold,
In the winter's embrace.

Shadows of the Ice Realm

Ice crystals catch the light,
Casting shadows on the ground,
In the stillness, they sound,
Whispers of magic bright.

Dancing in the moon's gleam,
Figures flicker and fade,
Each movement serenade,
In a cold, wondrous dream.

As the night stretches long,
The air sparkles and glows,
With secrets that it knows,
Echoing winter's song.

Silent tales unfold here,
In quiet corners bright,
Where shadows steal the night,
Wrapping dreams, pure and clear.

So let this space hold still,
Remember what has been,
For in shadows unseen,
Lies magic, pure and real.

Glittering Winter's Touch

Snowflakes fall, soft and light,
Each one a work of art,
A miracle to start,
Glittering through the night.

The world is wrapped in white,
With a blanket of dreams,
Each flake catching moonbeams,
In a calm, peaceful sight.

We wander through the woods,
Footsteps crunch on the ground,
In this hush all around,
Nature's beauty floods.

A chill sings through the air,
Yet warmth glows from within,
As we share in this win,
Moments precious and rare.

With each breath of the day,
We cherish winter's touch,
In its beauty, so much,
Guides us on our way.

Icicle Serenade

Hanging from eaves, a crystal song,
Dripping echoes, the winter's throng.
Glistening drops in the fading light,
Nature's choir, silent and bright.

Chiming gently with each soft breeze,
Whispers of cold through shivering trees.
A melody spun from the frosted air,
Icicles dance with a frosty flair.

Beneath the weight of a silent night,
Dreams of warmth spark with delight.
In the stillness, reflections play,
An icy serenade leads the way.

As dawn arrives, the song will fade,
Yet in the heart, the echoes stayed.
A fleeting glimpse, a breathless sigh,
Life's fragile beauty, hang and fly.

Ethereal Frosted Prism

Through the mist, a prism glows,
Colors twirl where the cold wind blows.
Whispers of ice in a soft embrace,
Nature's art, a fragile grace.

Delicate shapes of gleaming white,
Dreams transformed in the morning light.
Each facet catches the spark within,
A silent beauty that draws us in.

Frozen streams in radiant hues,
Dancing lightly with winter's muse.
A canvas laid beneath a moon,
Echoes of winter's soft, sweet tune.

As shadows linger and moments pass,
Time's gentle touch on the frosted glass.
In every breath, a lingering dream,
A prism born from winter's theme.

Luminous Winter's Embrace

In the twilight of an icy realm,
Light cascades, the dark to helm.
Snowflakes shimmer, a million stars,
Winter's touch, a dance of scars.

A blanket soft as whispered sighs,
Holding warmth where the chill denies.
Every flake tells a tale untold,
Of whispered dances in nights so cold.

Beneath the moon's argent glow,
Luminous paths the frost will show.
Embraced by silence, wrapped in white,
Winter's lullaby fades into night.

Through frozen air, the heart will leap,
In this embrace, the soul will keep.
Moments glimmer, like candles bright,
In the heart of winter's light.

The Dance of the Cold Light

Under the veil of a silver sky,
The frost takes flight, a gentle sigh.
Every shimmer a story's spark,
Carved in ice from the warmth of dark.

Whirling softly, shadows entwine,
Cold light dances in a graceful line.
Each breath a plume, a frosty waltz,
In the silence, no fear, no faults.

The earth adorned in a sparkling coat,
Beneath a sky where the snowflakes float.
In the air, a language pure,
The light of winter, soft and sure.

Round and round, the night unfolds,
In dazzling patterns, the story told.
With every blink, the magic stays,
The dance of light in winter's gaze.

Polar Twilight

The sky wears a cloak of night,
Stars twinkle with gentle light.
Whispers of frost in the air,
Nature rests without a care.

Mountains stand, silent and grand,
Palm fronds framed by snow-covered land.
Moonlight dances on the sea,
A serenade of tranquility.

Gleaming Echoes

In the forest, shadows play,
Echoes of the light of day.
Silver beams on ancient trees,
Rustling softly in the breeze.

A hidden path through emerald,
Stories of the wild retold.
Every whisper, every sound,
Nature's song, so profound.

Crystal Lattice

Sparkling forms where ice has grown,
Nature's art in structure sewn.
Each flake a unique design,
In winter's grasp, they intertwine.

A glistening world of pure delight,
Cascading hues in the soft twilight.
Fragile beauty, hard to hold,
Stories of warmth in the cold.

Silken Chill

Gentle whispers in the dark,
A cool breath leaves its mark.
Silk of night wraps all around,
In the stillness, peace is found.

A moment caught in icy breath,
Soft embraces, dance with death.
Serpentine shadows intertwine,
In this quiet, all is fine.

Whispering Glimmers

In twilight's soft embrace, they shine,
Flickering hopes, so divine.
A dance of stars upon the ground,
Whispers of magic all around.

Gentle breezes, secrets told,
In every glimmer, dreams unfold.
A world reborn in silver light,
Where shadows play and hearts take flight.

Through the trees, the soft winds sigh,
Underneath the vast, dark sky.
Each twinkle holds a silent wish,
A moment's pause, breathless bliss.

In the night, the echoes blend,
Harmony that will never end.
Promises hidden in the glow,
The beauty of the world we know.

As dawn approaches, glimmers fade,
Yet in our hearts, their warmth is laid.
We carry forth the night's embrace,
In every step, a quiet grace.

Rhythms of the Freeze

The world is hushed, like time stands still,
A melody that gives a thrill.
Under layers of glistening frost,
Whispers of warmth, yet never lost.

Every flake, a note of the song,
In symphony where hearts belong.
Crisp air dances, sparks ignite,
Painting dreams in black and white.

The ground cracks soft beneath our feet,
Nature's rhythm, cool and sweet.
With every step, we find our way,
In winter's arms, we choose to stay.

Trees adorned with icy lace,
Embrace the chill, this sacred space.
Here, in silence, beauty thrives,
In frozen moments, love survives.

As the sun dips low, shadows grow,
The world transformed, a wondrous show.
In the freeze, a pulse we chase,
Finding joy in this still place.

Winter's Crystal Serenade

Beneath the sky of icy blue,
A symphony of crystal dew.
Each note resounds in the still night,
A serenade of pure delight.

Snowflakes dance in tender grace,
With every breath, a warm embrace.
Echoes ring from distant trees,
Filling hearts with winter's ease.

Glittering valleys, fairytales spun,
As day meets night, two worlds are one.
In frosty air, our laughter soars,
A melody that freely pours.

The moon, a maestro in the dark,
Guides the song with a silver spark.
Every whisper, every sigh,
Reveals the magic passing by.

Harmony flows, a gentle tide,
Drawing us near, hearts open wide.
In winter's hug, we find our way,
A crystal serenade will stay.

Moonlight on the Snow

Softly glows the moon above,
Bathing earth in tender love.
Whispers travel on the breeze,
Filling nights with tranquil ease.

Shadows dance on fields so white,
A dreamscape formed in silver light.
Each step crunches, crisp and clear,
In this moment, all is near.

Reflecting dreams on frozen ground,
Voices of winter gather 'round.
The world at peace, serene and slow,
As moonlight paints the purest glow.

In the stillness, hearts align,
With every glimmer, souls combine.
Nature breathes, a gentle sigh,
Underneath the vast starry sky.

In the hush, connection grows,
As love and light in beauty flows.
Moonlight dreams upon the snow,
Whispers linger, ebb and flow.

Mystic Shard

In shadows deep, a light will gleam,
A shard of hope, a whispered dream.
It pierces through the night's embrace,
Reflecting truth with gentle grace.

The mystic glow, it dances bright,
Guiding souls through endless night.
Each spark a wish, a guiding star,
Illuminating paths from afar.

In silence soft, the echoes call,
Of ancient whispers, one and all.
Each shard, a story, yet untold,
In every glimmer, secrets bold.

Together we shall find our way,
Through mystic shards where shadows play.
With hearts aligned, we shall ascend,
In unity, our spirits blend.

So trust the light that breaks the dark,
For in the shard, ignites the spark.
A journey vast, a realm to chart,
The mystic shard, the weary heart.

Nebulous Frost

A veil of mist, the world a dream,
In nebulous frost, we softly gleam.
The morning light, a whispered sigh,
As winter's breath twirls through the sky.

Each crystal flake, a fleeting glance,
A dance of whites, a silent trance.
In nature's hush, the wonders rest,
Embracing all in wintry vest.

The frozen air, it sparkles bright,
As twilight brings the stars to light.
In moonlit nights, the shadows fade,
While magic weaves through every glade.

From frosty breath, the dreams arise,
In nebulous frost, beneath the skies.
The softest touch, a gentle chill,
A spell of peace, our hearts to fill.

So let us wander, hand in hand,
Through frosted fields, a wondrous land.
In every breath, a tale unfolds,
In nebulous frost, life gently holds.

Icy Halo

Around the moon, a halo bright,
Icy rings weave through the night.
A mystic circle, pure and round,
In silver dreams, the world is found.

Each glimmer bends the stars above,
A whisper soft, the night's sweet love.
With every breath, the cold ignites,
A dance of shadows, dreamy flights.

In icy stillness, all is calm,
The heart feels peace, a soothing balm.
As stars align in cosmic flow,
The halo's glow begins to show.

Through winter's grasp, we find the light,
In icy halo, soft and bright.
With hope anew, the dawn shall break,
As night retreats, the shadows shake.

So walk with me through winter's night,
In icy halo, souls take flight.
With every step, a path is paved,
In shimmering light, our hearts are saved.

Crystalline Melodies

In forests deep, the echoes play,
Crystalline melodies drift away.
Each note a glimpse, a fleeting sound,
In nature's hand, lost, yet found.

The wind it carries, soft and clear,
A symphony for those who hear.
Through rustling leaves and flowing stream,
The world awakes from a waking dream.

With every chime, the heart will sing,
As light cascades from everything.
In magical notes, we're swept along,
A harmony of life so strong.

The branches sway, the waters flow,
With crystalline charms, a vibrant show.
In fleeting moments, joy will bloom,
Resonating through the highest room.

So close your eyes and let it be,
Embrace the sound, feel wild and free.
In crystalline melodies, life's refrain,
A universe of love unchained.

Light Across the Frozen Expanse

A soft glow breaks the night,
Casting shadows on the frost.
Whispers of light take flight,
Across the expanse, never lost.

Stars twinkle in the cold,
Guiding paths to wander wide.
Silent stories yet untold,
As the universe does abide.

Moonbeams dance on icy streams,
Reflecting dreams of bright delight.
Nature's canvas softly schemes,
Painting wonders in the night.

A breath of chill in the air,
Frosty crystals twirl and glide.
A tranquil beauty, rich and rare,
In this vastness, we confide.

Light shines through the frozen veil,
A fleeting moment, pure and grand.
In its beauty, hearts prevail,
Across the quiet, shimmering land.

Celestial Ice Dance

Underneath the shimmering sky,
Dancing lights in the frozen air.
Orbs of ice that twirl and fly,
In a waltz, they swirl with flair.

The night hums a gentle tune,
Stars participate in the show.
Whispers float like petals strewn,
As the chilly breezes blow.

Glistening crystals take their flight,
Moonlit echoes softly chime.
Nature's art in the pale light,
Captures hearts in fleeting rhyme.

Beneath the glow, the world is hushed,
All is calm, the pulse is slow.
In this realm, no rush, no crush,
Just the dance of ice and glow.

Celestial bodies share their grace,
As shadows melt in bright romance.
In this moment, find your place,
Join the ethereal ice dance.

Frost-kissed Splendor

In dawn's embrace, the world awakes,
Frost-kissed splendor all around.
Nature sparkles, beauty makes,
A silent symphony profound.

Icicles hang like crystal tears,
Glistening in the morning light.
Each droplet holds our hopes and fears,
Reflecting dreams, both bold and bright.

Beneath the branches draped in white,
Whispers of winter softly sigh.
In every corner, pure delight,
As snowflakes drift gently by.

The earth wears a robe of sheen,
Every horizon gleams with grace.
A canvas brushed in silver sheen,
Invites the wanderers to trace.

Frost-kissed moments, fleeting fast,
In each sparkle, memories blend.
In nature's arms, we feel the vast,
Embracing splendor without end.

Frozen Glimmers

In the stillness of the night,
Frozen glimmers catch the eye.
Every crystal holds the light,
Underneath the boundless sky.

A tapestry of silver threads,
Woven through the arms of trees.
Nature whispers, softly spreads,
Magic dances in the breeze.

Each glimmer tells a tale anew,
Of chilly dreams and warmth inside.
A flicker of the world so true,
Where heart and silence coincide.

The frosty ground beneath our feet,
Echoes of a soft delight.
Surrounded by this wintry sheet,
We find serenity in sight.

In every shimmer, hope is found,
A reminder of the beauty near.
In frozen glimmers all around,
Our spirits lift, our joys appear.

Veil of Winter's Light

A soft glow breaks the dawn,
Blanketing earth in white.
Whispers of snow gently fall,
Crystals dance in winter's light.

Branches bend with heavy grace,
Laden with their frosty crowns.
Silent are the frozen paths,
Winds weave tales of snowy towns.

Echoes of the night remain,
Stars glint like scattered ice.
The world wrapped in peaceful dreams,
Underneath this cold, clear guise.

Children laugh and chase the flakes,
Life returns with joy and cheer.
Breath clouds linger in the air,
Filling hearts with warmth, sincere.

With each breath, the magic hums,
In this season, still and bright.
Veil of winter softly drapes,
A cloak of pure, enchanted light.

Window to an Icy World

Through frosted panes I see,
An enchanting, still display.
Nature holds her breath, so calm,
In a world of shade and gray.

Icicles hang like silver swords,
Glistening in the morning sun.
Each branch is etched with stories told,
Of winter's reign and how it's spun.

Footsteps crunch on frozen ground,
The stillness sings a quiet song.
Time seems halted in its flight,
In this realm where dreams belong.

The sky bends low, a muted hue,
Clouds draped in chilly, whispering sighs.
A window to this icy world,
Where every moment, magic lies.

As day fades into evening's arms,
Stars emerge to light the frost.
In this space, serenity reigns,
A treasure found, not easily lost.

Glistening Grasp

Morning dew on blades of grass,
Sparkles like a million gems.
Nature's art in purest form,
Crafted with her finest stems.

The air is crisp, the silence deep,
Nature's heartbeat, soft and slow.
Fingers reach for glistening leaves,
In a world where wonders grow.

Sunlight filters through the trees,
Casting shadows, rich and wide.
Every droplet tells a tale,
Of whispers where the secrets hide.

Time bursts forth in fleeting hues,
Each moment caught in amber's glance.
A tapestry of frost and sun,
In nature's ever-glistening dance.

Breathe in deeply, feel it wrap,
Around your soul, a tender clasp.
In nature's arms, let worries cease,
Within her glistening, tender grasp.

Frosted Poetry

Words are etched upon the air,
Whispers woven, soft and clear.
Frosted verses, delicate touch,
Each line a note for hearts to hear.

Snowflakes drift, like thoughts in flight,
Dancing gently, fleeting grace.
In the hush of winter's night,
Poetic dreams begin to trace.

Nature's canvas, vast and white,
Brushstrokes of the chilly breeze.
Frosty letters form a rhyme,
A symphony of shivers, ease.

Underneath the silver sky,
Echoes of frozen tales unfold.
Frosted poetry, a gentle art,
Unraveled tales of warmth and cold.

In this moment, breathe it in,
Let every word embrace your soul.
Winter's ink flows from the heart,
Creating beauty in the whole.

Glistening Silence

In the hush of dawn's first light,
Snowflakes fall, a pure delight.
Every whisper, soft and clear,
Glistening silence draws us near.

Footsteps echo on the street,
Nature's blanket, soft and sweet.
Time stands still, a sacred pause,
In winter's grasp, we find our cause.

Frosted branches, gleaming bright,
An ethereal, crystal sight.
In the stillness, dreams take flight,
Carried forth in pure delight.

Candles flicker in the glow,
Hearts entwined in gentle flow.
Moments linger, softly blend,
In this silence, we transcend.

With each breath, the world feels new,
In the calm, we find our true.
Glistening silence, hold me tight,
In your arms, all feels just right.

Twilight on the Ice

Beneath the skies of dusky hue,
The fading light, a peaceful view.
Reflections dance on icy glass,
As day gives way, the moments pass.

Footprints sketch a fleeting mark,
Whispers travel through the dark.
Twilight's kiss upon the lake,
A gentle breath, the stillness wakes.

Stars emerge, a sparkling crew,
In silent skies, their light rings true.
The world enveloped in a dream,
A silver laugh, a quiet gleam.

Shadows stretch and slowly creep,
As nature settles down to sleep.
In this twilight, hearts unite,
Wrapped in warmth, holding tight.

Let time dissolve in this embrace,
As twilight paints the perfect space.
Together here, we find our way,
A soft goodbye to fading day.

A Coat of Frost

Nature dons her frosty gown,
Dewdrops glisten, melting down.
Each blade of grass, a jeweled thread,
In morning light, our worries shed.

A sparkle here, a shimmer there,
Every corner, whispers rare.
Underneath the arching trees,
Frosty patterns dance in breeze.

The world transformed, a snowy dream,
Every surface, a gentle gleam.
With every touch, the coolness spreads,
Painting whispers where we tread.

A canvas bright, a work of art,
Winter's chill warms every heart.
In this beauty, we find peace,
A coat of frost, our sweet release.

Together, in this fleeting hour,
We marvel at winter's power.
A moment caught, forever stays,
With every breath, we sing our praise.

Dappled Sun on Frozen Ground

Sunlight spills through branches bare,
Dancing patterns, light and air.
Each moment flickers, fades away,
As winter whispers soft ballet.

A world adorned in icy lace,
Every shadow finds its place.
In the stillness, warmth breaks through,
Dappled sun, a golden hue.

Footsteps crunch on snow so bright,
Echoes of a winter's flight.
Nature's canvas, bold and vast,
Solitude, our shadows cast.

The frozen ground holds stories told,
In glimmers of a world of gold.
Hearts awaken, spirit soars,
In the sunlight, winter roars.

Beneath the chill, we find the light,
In every moment, pure delight.
Dappled sun on frozen ground,
In this beauty, love is found.

The Silent Glitter

In the night, stars gleam bright,
Whispers dance in the air's light.
Dreams unfold beneath the sky,
Silent glitters, floating by.

Moonlit paths where shadows glide,
Secrets held, where hearts confide.
Softly glows the twilight's art,
Silent whispers, a tender heart.

In the dark, magic flows wide,
Each twinkle tells of joy inside.
Stillness reigns, yet spirits soar,
Silent glitters, forevermore.

Underneath the vast expanse,
Hope emerges, sparks a chance.
With each beat, the silence sings,
A treasure born from hidden things.

Trust the night, it holds the key,
Unlocks the heart for all to see.
In this glow, our dreams unite,
Silent glitters, pure delight.

Sparkle on the Surface

On the lake, the sun does play,
Ripples dance in bright array.
Each small wave, a fleeting gem,
Sparkle shines, a diadem.

Life reflects in tranquil waves,
Capturing what the moment saves.
Every luster, a golden trace,
Sparkle lingers, time and space.

Beneath the ripples, depth resides,
Mysteries where silence hides.
With each glance, a story told,
Sparkle glimmers, purest gold.

In the breeze, soft echoes call,
Nature's canvas, embracing all.
Floating dreams upon the tide,
Sparkle whispers, love and pride.

Amidst the calm, the heart can tell,
Beauty found in its own shell.
Dance along the water's face,
Sparkle on, with gentle grace.

Frigid Spark

Amidst the frost, a shimmer glows,
In the chill, a fire flows.
Frigid air, crisp and bright,
A spark ignites, pierces night.

Snowflakes fall, a silent show,
Each one unique, a chance to grow.
In the quiet, warmth may spark,
Frigid touch ignites the dark.

Through the cold, spirits rise,
Dreams ascend to painted skies.
Even in the bitter freeze,
Frigid sparks can bring us peace.

With each breath, a frost-kissed sigh,
Awakens flame that won't deny.
In the stillness, hearts ignite,
Frigid spark, our guiding light.

Winter's breath, a fleeting kiss,
In the chill, we find our bliss.
From the cold, the warmth will part,
Frigid spark within the heart.

Icy Dances

On the lake, the ice does gleam,
Winter's touch, a frozen dream.
Beneath the stars, shadows prance,
Nature's beauty, icy dance.

Whispers glide on frosty air,
Footprints mark where hearts laid bare.
Glinting patterns twirling free,
Icy dances, joy's decree.

With every swirl, the silence reigns,
Nature's rhythm, soft refrains.
Delicate steps, the world unfolds,
Icy dances, stories told.

Underneath the frozen sky,
Joyful laughter, soaring high.
In this moment, lose the trance,
Icy wonders, hearts enhance.

With each twirl, the night aligns,
All is magic when love shines.
In the still, a chance to prance,
Icy dances, life's romance.

The Glow of Winter

The moonlight casts a silver hue,
As snowflakes dance on winds that blew.
The world is wrapped in quiet dreams,
Beneath the glow, a peace redeems.

The branches wear a lace of white,
Glistening softly in the night.
Each breath a cloud, a fleeting sigh,
As stars above begin to fly.

In shadows deep, the whispers call,
Of winter's charm, enchanting all.
With every step, the crunching sound,
A melody of frost profound.

The fires burn with warmth and cheer,
Families gather, hearts draw near.
Stories shared beneath the glow,
In winter's arms, love starts to grow.

The dawn will bring a crisp anew,
With colors bright, the sky turns blue.
Yet in this stillness, we will find,
The glow of winter, sweetly kind.

Diamond Dust in Snow

Upon the ground, a purest light,
Sparkles like jewels, a wondrous sight.
Each flake a gem, unique and clear,
A blanket soft, winter's frontier.

The gentle breeze, it stirs the air,
Whispers of dreams in the frosty snare.
In silence deep, the world stands still,
As nature wraps in a sparkling thrill.

Children laugh as they twirl and play,
In fields of white, where shadows lay.
Their joy ignites the crystal glow,
In diamond dust, the magic flows.

The evening falls, the stars appear,
With twinkling lights that bring good cheer.
As night draws close with gentle grace,
The diamond dust finds its place.

In winter's clutch, we find delight,
In all the beauty, pure and bright.
With every flake, a promise grows,
Forever cherished, this world of snow.

Frosted Tints

The dawn reveals a world transformed,
In frosted tints, the earth adorned.
Each blade of grass wears crystal lace,
A beauty found in nature's embrace.

The trees stand tall, their branches bare,
Draped in white, a vision rare.
The colors blend, from blue to grey,
As winter paints the world display.

A frozen pond, a shiny sheet,
Reflecting skies where soft winds meet.
Ice dances lightly on the skin,
In frosted tints, the wonder spins.

The air is laced with chilly bite,
Yet warms the heart with pure delight.
As fires crackle, stories weave,
In frosted tints, we dare believe.

With every twilight's gentle fade,
A palette soft that winter made.
The beauty lies in subtle hints,
In every shade of frosted tints.

Radiant Winter Tapestry

A tapestry of white and blue,
Woven with threads of crisp and new.
In every stitch, a story told,
Of winter's grip, of nights so cold.

The sun peeks through the clouded veil,
Casting warmth on the snowy trail.
Each flake a piece of art divine,
In radiant glow, they intertwine.

The mountain tops wear crowns of frost,
While rivers whisper, not a sound lost.
Nature unfolds her grand design,
In every glimmer, a hidden sign.

Beneath the stars, the silence sings,
As winter spreads her gentle wings.
In the night's embrace, dreams take flight,
A radiant tapestry, pure delight.

So let us bask in winter's grace,
With every breath, we find our place.
In this grand weave of softest light,
The heart finds joy in winter's night.

Radiant Frostwork

Lace of ice on windowpane,
Dancing light, like winter's reign.
Whispers soft in chilled embrace,
Nature's touch, an artful grace.

Glistening trees in silver hue,
Sparkling dreams of frosty dew.
Morning's breath, a crystal sigh,
As time drifts gently, passing by.

Footprints whisper on the ground,
Silent echoes all around.
Branches bow beneath the weight,
Of frostwork spun with tender fate.

Each flake falls, a silent flight,
Crafting echoes, pure delight.
In this world of white and blue,
Magic stirs in all that's true.

With every breath, the chill we share,
A fleeting moment, sweet and rare.
In winter's grasp, we're held so tight,
In radiant frostwork, purest light.

The Art of Cold

Brush of winter, soft and light,
Painting dreams in shades of white.
Each crisp morn, a canvas new,
The art of cold, a view askew.

Frozen streams and crystal nights,
Whispers echo in the heights.
Nature's palette, pure and clear,
A frosty vision drawing near.

Snowflakes twirl in graceful dance,
Enchanting beauty, a fleeting glance.
Stars above in silent gaze,
Sparkle softly, night's sweet praise.

The world in stillness, hush profound,
In every breath, a subtle sound.
Time stands still, as moments fold,
Revealing gently, the art of cold.

In this realm where dreams take flight,
We find solace, warmth from night.
Amidst the chill, our spirits soar,
In cold's embrace, forevermore.

Diaphanous Winter

Veils of white, so soft and thin,
Whispered tales where dreams begin.
In the hush of falling flakes,
Winter weaves, as silence breaks.

Gentle winds with secrets pass,
Through the woods, on mirrored glass.
Each breath lingers, crisp and bright,
In diaphanous, purest light.

Shadows dance in muted glow,
As twilight wraps the world in snow.
Stars peek through a silver veil,
In winter's grip, soft stories sail.

Quiet lakes in icy hush,
Lend their hearts to winter's brush.
Across the land, a dreamer's shimmer,
In gentle light, our hopes grow dimmer.

Those fleeting moments, soft and rare,
Together bond us, made to share.
In diaphanous winter's hold,
Our hearts unite, as warmth unfolds.

Frigid Halo

In the stillness, shadows play,
Frigid halo lights the way.
Frosted edges touch the dawn,
As the chill begins to yawn.

Glimmers twine in chilly air,
Woven tales of frost laid bare.
Nature's breath, a quiet sigh,
Underneath the pale blue sky.

Each crystal spark, a fleeting dream,
Echoes soft, like whispered beams.
In the night, the stars align,
To frame the world, a frozen design.

Paths of white, where whispers roam,
In this winter, we find home.
Frigid halos, bright and clear,
Guide us near, to what we hold dear.

Embrace the cold, let it sweep
Through our hearts, as secrets keep.
In every flake, a story told,
Of life and love, in frigid cold.

Reflections in the Frost

A morning cloak of icy sheen,
Mirrors dreams in silvery gleam.
Threads of light weave through the trees,
Nature holds her breath with ease.

Crystal patterns, delicate lace,
Whispers of winter's soft embrace.
Each breath hangs like fragile art,
A dance of chill that warms the heart.

Footprints pressed on frosty ground,
In quiet wonder, peace is found.
The world reflects a still embrace,
A moment held in time and space.

The sun peeks through the azure sky,
Kisses the frost, a gentle sigh.
In the hush, the world seems to pause,
Capturing beauty without cause.

As day unfolds, the frost will fade,
Yet memories in hearts are laid.
In sparkling glints of morning light,
Reflections linger, pure and bright.

Frosty Whispers of Light

A whisper travels through the trees,
Frosty kisses on the breeze.
Glimmers dance on branches bare,
Nature's secrets linger there.

Shadows fall on frosted ground,
Silence reigns, no other sound.
Each breath, a cloud of gentle white,
In the arms of quiet night.

Morning breaks with colors bold,
Frosted tales of wonder told.
Light beacons through the icy air,
A symphony, so soft and rare.

Frozen dreams in every hue,
The landscape framed with morning dew.
Frosty whispers, sweet and clear,
Softly echo, drawing near.

As daylight warms the winter chill,
New horizons promise will.
In every sparkle, life ignites,
Frosty moments, pure delights.

Twilight's Icy Glow

The twilight descends, a gentle sigh,
With flickers of stars that twinkle high.
Icy rays dance on twilight's breath,
A pathway carved from light and death.

Moonlight cradles the earth in white,
Casting shadows that stretch in the night.
Whispers of calm fill the air,
The world suspended, devoid of care.

Chill winds beckon with soft caress,
Frosty gems in a silken dress.
Nature sleeps, wrapped in her coat,
Amidst the glow, dreams softly float.

Each flake a story, a tale retold,
In the silence, magic unfolds.
Twilight glimmers, casting its spell,
In the icy hush, all is well.

As night deepens, secrets arise,
Under the watchful, starlit skies.
With every breath, the beauty grows,
In twilight's arms, where stillness flows.

Enchanted Frost

In the stillness, frost takes form,
Painting landscapes that feel warm.
Each breath of air, a whisper fine,
Nature's magic, a grand design.

Crystals sparkle like diamonds bright,
Holding secrets of the night.
Branches wear a cloak of ice,
Every corner, a paradise.

The world transformed in silver light,
Enchanting dreams that take flight.
Echoes linger with every thought,
In this realm, the heart is caught.

Moonlit paths of glistening white,
Guiding souls through peaceful night.
In this wonderland we roam,
Frosted magic feels like home.

When dawn arrives, the world will change,
Yet the beauty feels so strange.
But in hearts, the frost remains,
Enchanted visions, sweet refrains.

Cascades of Crystal

Water tumbles down the stone,
Shimmering light, a glistening tone.
Beneath the trees, they softly fall,
Nature's voice, a gentle call.

Rainbows dance in droplets pure,
Each cascade, an art so sure.
Whispers carried on the breeze,
A tranquil symphony with ease.

Silken streams weave through the glen,
Binding earth and sky again.
Softly echoing through the night,
The crystal paths reflect the light.

Mountains cradle dreams so high,
Beneath the vast and starry sky.
Where water sings in pure delight,
The world awakes to morning light.

In every splash, a story told,
Of secret journeys, brave and bold.
Cascades of crystal, whisper clear,
In nature's heart, we find our cheer.

Echoes of the Frosted Night

Moonlit skies in silver glow,
Blanket the world, gentle and slow.
Frosty whispers fill the air,
A chilly charm, beyond compare.

Stars wink softly from afar,
Guiding dreams with their bright spar.
Underneath a frozen veil,
Quiet magic weaves its tale.

Trees adorned in crystalline,
Nature's artwork, pure and fine.
Each breath visible, a fleeting sight,
Echoes dance in the frosted night.

A hush enfolds the sleeping land,
Whispers soft as a lover's hand.
In this stillness, hearts unite,
Bound by echoes of the night.

With every step, the ground does creak,
In frozen realms, the night speaks.
A fleeting glimpse, a moment's grace,
In frosted dreams, we find our place.

The Gloss of Silence

Silence blankets the waking dawn,
In stillness, worries are withdrawn.
A world untouched by the noise,
Wrapped in peace, the heart enjoys.

Still waters beneath the trees,
Whisper secrets carried on the breeze.
Calm reflections dance and sway,
In the gloss of silence, we stay.

Quiet moments, time stands still,
A tranquil grace, a soothing thrill.
Nature hums its gentle song,
In this quiet, we belong.

Waves of calm caress the shore,
In silent depths, we explore more.
The hush envelops, soft and deep,
In the gloss of silence, we reap.

Every sigh, a breath of peace,
In soft shadows, our worries cease.
The world speaks softly, whispers clear,
In silence, we find what is dear.

Glistening Echoes

Morning dew upon the grass,
Glistening jewels, moments pass.
Each droplet catches the sun's embrace,
Reflecting light in a gentle grace.

Echoes of nature's quiet song,
Fill the air, where dreams belong.
A sunbeam dances on a stream,
Painting the world with a golden beam.

Whispers of wind through the leaves,
In every turn, the spirit believes.
Stories told by the rustling trees,
Glistening echoes on the breeze.

The mountain's majesty stands tall,
With shining peaks, a call for all.
Nature's beauty, vast and wide,
In glistening echoes, we abide.

As twilight falls, the stars ignite,
Guiding us through the coming night.
Their glimmering tales weave through the dark,
In glistening echoes, we find our spark.

Glimmering Solstice

The sun dips low, a golden hue,
Whispers of warmth, a dance anew.
Long shadows blend with twilight's grace,
Hearts embrace the light's embrace.

Stars awaken in the starlit dome,
Each one sparkles, calling us home.
Nature sings a soft, sweet tune,
As day gives way to silver moon.

Flickering candles, soft and bright,
Guide us gently through the night.
Silent wishes fill the air,
In this moment, we dare to care.

In the chill, love's warmth ignites,
Turning darkness into sights.
Together we weave our dreams so bold,
In the magic of stories told.

Awakening hope, we stand as one,
Chasing shadows 'til the dawn.
With each heartbeat, joy will soar,
A glimmering solstice, forevermore.

Tinsel Tundra

Snowflakes fall like bits of lace,
Covering the world with grace.
Hoarfrost kisses every tree,
A shimmering tapestry.

Icicles hang like crystal spears,
Guarding secrets of the years.
Footprints whisper in the white,
Marking paths through the night.

In the stillness, spirits gleam,
Wrapped in warmth like a cozy dream.
Fires crackle, hearths aglow,
As winds continue their soft flow.

Tinsel drapes from branches low,
Twinkling softly in the snow.
Joy and laughter fill the air,
In this winter wonder, we share.

A sled glides down a slope so steep,
Echoing laughter, memories to keep.
In this tinsel tundra bright and fair,
Love's embrace lingers everywhere.

Crystalized Secrets

In the depths where shadows lie,
Secrets whisper, softly sigh.
In the dark, the truth unfolds,
Stories waiting to be told.

Crystal shards of dreams once bright,
Sparkle faintly in the night.
Every glimmer holds a key,
Unlocking chains of mystery.

Echoes of laughter, hints of tears,
Capture echoes of our fears.
Fragments glisten, tales concealed,
In the heart, their fate revealed.

With every breath, we seek to find,
The hidden treasures left behind.
In the silence, we must delve,
To uncover the truths we shelve.

Crystalized in moments rare,
Life's essence woven with care.
Through the glass, we gaze and see,
The beauty of our destiny.

A Symphony of Glare

Lights dance brightly in the night,
A symphony of vivid light.
Colors bloom and shadows play,
Chasing darkness far away.

In the chaos, harmony found,
Through the noise, a sweeter sound.
Beats that pulse within the soul,
As every moment takes its toll.

Glistening beams turn the mundane,
Each reflection softly refrains.
Life's rhythm, a tender guide,
Within the glow, we shall abide.

Melodies rise on currents high,
Echoing dreams that fill the sky.
Together, we dance and twirl,
In a dazzling, vibrant whirl.

A symphony of smiles and flare,
Boundless joy scattered everywhere.
In this orchestra, we share,
The beauty woven in the glare.

Shattered Chills

The wind whispers low, cold and near,
Quiet secrets that only we hear.
Crystals glisten on the frozen ground,
Each step shatters, a haunting sound.

Moonlight dances on the icy slate,
Shivering shadows, we hesitate.
Breath taken, in the frosty air,
Moments frozen, a silent prayer.

Branches groan with a heavy frost,
Life suspended, counting the cost.
Winter's breath upon the barren trees,
Chill claws at us, a bitter breeze.

A world transformed in silver and gray,
Echoes of laughter drift far away.
Each heartbeat quickens in the black night,
Searching for warmth, for a flicker of light.

Shattered dreams in the cold moon's gaze,
Counting the nights, in the winter haze.
Yet in the darkness, a flicker shines,
Hope warms the heart as the cold reclines.

A Canvas of Crystals

Nature's brush paints the world anew,
With icy strokes, a glorious view.
Sunrise glimmers on the snowy plains,
A canvas shimmering, beauty reigns.

Each flake falls like a whispered dream,
Twinkling softly in the morning beam.
Patterns form in the layers of white,
A masterpiece forged in winter's light.

Trees don crowns of intricate frost,
Delicate jewels, never lost.
Winter's splendor, a fleeting art,
Captured moments that warm the heart.

As twilight falls, the canvas glows,
Under the stars, a story flows.
Every crystal tells a tale of old,
In silence speaks, where dreams unfold.

Painting the night in a chill embrace,
A world transformed, a timeless space.
In this frozen art, we find our way,
In a canvas of crystals, we choose to stay.

The Mosaic of Winter

Fragments of ice and shards of light,
Create a world so pure and bright.
Every corner holds a magic spell,
Whispers of stories only time can tell.

Snowflakes dance like whispers soft,
Gentle breezes lift them aloft.
Together they weave a tapestry,
Of winter's touch, wild and free.

Patterns shift in the moonlit glow,
Each piece harmonizes, row by row.
A mosaic rich with color and hue,
Nature's work, in pristine view.

Beneath the stars, we walk the lines,
Of sparkling dreams where winter shines.
A journey through this frozen land,
Holding each moment within our hand.

As dawn breaks gently, colors meld,
The mosaic shifts, beauty upheld.
In winter's grip, we find our grace,
In the mosaic, our hearts embrace.

A Chill in the Air

The leaves have started falling low,
A whisper of winter's gentle flow.
The breath of dusk, a frosty sigh,
As twilight paints the cobalt sky.

The trees stand bare, their limbs like lace,
In every corner, a still embrace.
Footsteps crunch on pathways clear,
Echoing softly, winter is near.

The air is crisp, a sharp delight,
Stars emerge in the velvet night.
The moon hangs low, a frosty pearl,
In this enchanting, quiet world.

The chill invites a cozy space,
Warm blankets wrapped, a soft embrace.
Hot cocoa steams on the table set,
Memories linger I shan't forget.

With every gust, the moment glows,
In this serene, soft silence flows.
A chill in the air, a sweet refrain,
A winter's song, the heart's domain.

Enchanted by the Frost

In morning's light, the frost awakens,
Each blade of grass with diamonds shaken.
Nature dressed in shimmering white,
A wonderland, pure and bright.

The rooftops wear a crystal crown,
While shadows stretch across the town.
A breath of magic fills the day,
Enchanted realms in bright array.

Footprints linger in the frozen dew,
While the sun breaks forth, a warming hue.
Children laugh, their cheeks aglow,
In this frosty dance, they twirl and flow.

Luminous trees with branches bare,
Hold secrets whispered on the air.
A stillness reigns, a moment caught,
In shadows deep, enchantment wrought.

The world transformed, a fairy's bliss,
In every flake, a subtle kiss.
Enchanted by the frost we see,
The beauty hidden, wild and free.

The Quiet Radiance

As daylight dims and shadows blend,
A glowing warmth begins to send.
The quiet radiance fills the space,
In golden hues, it finds its grace.

Whispers of dusk in tender tones,
Rustling leaves, the softest moans.
Every corner softly lit,
With peaceful glow, the world will sit.

Candles flicker with a gentle hand,
A flicker of light across the land.
In the stillness, hearts relate,
To the beauty, calm, and fate.

Stars awaken in velvet skies,
Reflecting dreams with ancient sighs.
A quiet radiance shines so bright,
Illuminating the coming night.

In moments shared, in silence deep,
Connections forged, promises we keep.
The softest glow, a love so pure,
In quiet radiance, we endure.

Prismatic Chill

Morning breaks in a spectrum bright,
Colors dance in winter's light.
A prismatic chill fills the air,
As nature dons her bright cloak, rare.

The sun ignites the icy streams,
Painting edges with silver beams.
A symphony of colors bloom,
In every angle, whispers loom.

The frost-kissed ground, a patchwork quilt,
With vibrant hues of nature's built.
Each breath, a cloud, like art divine,
Suspended time, a quiet sign.

Branches glisten as sunlight bends,
In every turn, a magic lends.
A prismatic chill, heartstrings play,
In this wonderland, dreams find their way.

Nature's beauty, a fleeting dream,
In winter's grasp, a radiant beam.
With every shade, our spirits rise,
In the prismatic chill, we find our skies.

Frost's Gentle Touch

With softest breath, the night descends,
A silken veil that gently mends.
Each blade of grass in shimmer dressed,
In frost's embrace, the world finds rest.

The moonlight spills on twinkling hues,
Creating magic in the dew.
A world transformed, so calm, so still,
Nature's wonder, winter's thrill.

The trees wear crowns of sparkling ice,
Each branch adorned, a paradise.
Whispers carried on the breeze,
A frosty kiss that warms with ease.

The air is crisp, the silence deep,
While dreams in frozen beauty sweep.
In every corner, shadows play,
A winter's tale in soft display.

And as the dawn begins to break,
The frosted earth begins to wake.
Each shimmer fades, a brief hello,
To greet the sun, a gentle glow.

A Tapestry of Cold

A tapestry of white and blue,
Woven through the morning dew.
Each snowflake falls, a work of art,
As winter weaves its chilly heart.

Under the sky, a canvas wide,
The winds of change begin to glide.
Branches arch in a frosty bow,
Nature's breath is pure and low.

The frozen lake, a mirror bright,
Reflects the stars in the quiet night.
Whispers echo through the trees,
Carried softly on the breeze.

A shiver in the air, so light,
Encapsulates the quiet night.
A world adorned in crystal lace,
In winter's grip, we find our place.

As laughter floats on chilly air,
The joy of winter everywhere.
We gather close, our hearts entwined,
In this embrace, true warmth we find.

Twinkling in the Chill

Stars like diamonds dance above,
In the midnight chill, they move.
Each flicker tells a tale untold,
A secret shared, a dream to hold.

The night is dressed in silky hues,
Infusing magic in the blues.
Every breath a cloud of mist,
Moments passing, none dismissed.

With every step, the snowflakes sigh,
Underfoot as time drifts by.
In quiet corners, shadows creep,
While the world surrenders to sleep.

The frosty air, a crisp embrace,
Inviting smiles upon each face.
With laughter rising, joy fulfilled,
We cherish warmth as hearts are thrilled.

Through winter nights, our spirits soar,
Embracing all that lies in store.
Together, where the chill meets cheer,
The twinkling stars our dreams engineer.

Luminous Frostwork

Frostwork glistens, a pure delight,
Nature's craft in the morning light.
Each crystal formed, a delicate piece,
Whispering secrets of winter's fleece.

A landscape painted in silver and gray,
Where every shadow softly sways.
Sunrise breaks with a golden brush,
Illuminating the world in a hush.

The air is filled with sparkling charms,
Inviting all to open their arms.
Each frosty breath a gift we hold,
In this embrace, our stories told.

The grass beneath, a jeweled bed,
Where every step a tale is spread.
The beauty lies in the fleeting chill,
A moment captured, time stands still.

In winter's heart, we find our peace,
A luminous world that will not cease.
Together we dance in the glinting glow,
Where frosty dreams and love will flow.

Crystal Reflections

In the stillness of the night,
Mirrors of ice, pure and bright.
Whispers of dreams, softly flow,
Caught in a world of glimmering glow.

Each shard a song, a tale unfolds,
Of winter's breath and secrets told.
A dance of light on the frozen lake,
Where shadows linger, and echoes wake.

Facets of memory, sharp and clear,
Encapsulated wonders draw near.
In silence, they shimmer, in silence, they sing,
The beauty of winter, a jeweled offering.

Shifting and swirling, the crystals play,
As dawn's first light melts night away.
A fleeting moment, yet firmly set,
In the heart of the soul, we shan't forget.

With every glint, a story shines,
Of fleeting time and changing lines.
In crystal reflections, we find our peace,
As troubled thoughts and worries cease.

Dance of the Frost

Frosty whispers swirl in air,
Dancing lightly, without a care.
Each flake a story, unique and rare,
In the moonlight's tender glare.

They twirl like dancers, free and bold,
Painting the earth with silver and gold.
As night descends and shadows creep,
In winter's embrace, the world falls asleep.

A symphony soft, the silence hums,
While nature stirs, and the stillness drums.
With every flutter, each fleeting trace,
The dance of frost leaves a gentle grace.

Beneath the stars, they flutter anew,
A ballet of ice in the crisp night dew.
With laughter abound, they freeze in time,
The artistry of frost, a silent rhyme.

As dawn climbs high, with golden rays,
The dancers bow, the frost obeys.
Yet in our hearts, the memories stay,
Of the dance of frost, that brings the day.

Ethereal Fragments

Fragments of light in twilight's dream,
Gathering whispers, a soft moonbeam.
Through veils of mist, they gently glide,
Whispers of secrets the night can't hide.

Each fragment holds a tale untold,
Of lands unseen and hearts of gold.
In the silence, their beauty unfolds,
As time flows slowly, the world beholds.

Woven in starlight, the dreams take flight,
Carried aloft on the wings of night.
An ethereal glow that beckons near,
Painting the dark with warmth and cheer.

Through the shadows, they softly dance,
With a hint of magic, a fleeting chance.
In the tapestry of night, they blend,
Ethereal fragments that never end.

As dawn approaches, the light will wane,
Yet in our hearts, they shall remain.
A reminder sweet of the night's embrace,
With ethereal fragments, we find our place.

Chilled Radiance

In the quietude, a chill resides,
Draped in radiance, the winter hides.
Crystals twinkle, catching the light,
In the heart of the frost, a wondrous sight.

Each breath is visible, crisp and clear,
Echoing laughter we hold dear.
While the world waits in hushed delight,
Chilled radiance shines through the night.

Under starlit skies, magic flows,
Embracing the stillness, as nature knows.
In the frosty air, we take our stand,
Held by the beauty that graces the land.

With every step on the blanket of snow,
Our hearts beat softly, the warmth does grow.
For in chilled radiance, love will spur,
A gentle reminder, we are all one blur.

As dawn breaks gracefully over the hills,
The world awakens, and hope fulfills.
In chilled radiance, we find our way,
A treasure of light in a wintry display.

Luminous Chill

In the quiet of the night,
Stars twinkle with delight.
A breath of frosty air,
Whispers secrets everywhere.

Moonlight spills on silver ground,
Where dreams and shadows are found.
The world in a gentle haze,
Wrapped in winter's embracing gaze.

Footsteps crunch on crystal dust,
Every moment feels a must.
A shiver dances on skin,
As the magic tugs within.

Time seems to pause and sigh,
Underneath the vast, dark sky.
Each heartbeat a slow thrill,
In this luminous, chilling still.

Nature's breath, a soft sigh,
Underneath the starry eye.
In this world, we find our peace,
As the night gifts sweet release.

Icicle Symphony

Hanging from the eaves, they gleam,
Nature's orchestra, a dream.
Each drop a note in time,
A melody, crisp and sublime.

Shimmering in the morning light,
Icicles dance, a wondrous sight.
The air fills with their song,
As winter's anthem plays along.

Chimes of frost on a breeze,
Echo through the frosted trees.
With every shimmer and sway,
Nature's beauty on display.

Rivulets form and flow,
Composing a gentle show.
Harmony in the chill,
Icicles, frozen yet still.

Beneath the weight of white,
They glisten, pure and bright.
In silence, they enchant,
As winter's song takes a dance.

Dance of the Frozen Veil

In the frost, the whispers twirl,
Snowflakes fall, a delicate swirl.
Nature dons her icy dress,
In beauty wrapped, a silent caress.

Glimmers catch the falling light,
A dance of shadows, pure and bright.
The world becomes a canvas white,
In winter's grasp, a wondrous sight.

Glistening paths beneath our feet,
Where dreams and reality meet.
Each step a touch on nature's face,
A gentle waltz, a tender grace.

Underneath the frozen stars,
We trace our hopes and distant scars.
In this stillness, we regain,
The warmth that lingers through the pain.

Together in this icy dance,
We lose ourselves in the trance.
As nature weaves her subtle spell,
In the dance of the frozen veil.

Radiance in Stillness

Upon the lake, the moonlight lies,
A mirror for the starry skies.
Frozen ripples tell a tale,
A shimmering, quiet veil.

The world halts in peaceful grace,
In this frozen, tranquil space.
Every breath is a sacred sigh,
In stillness, hearts learn to fly.

Crystals bloom on branches bare,
Nature's jewels, rich and rare.
Each flake a memory spun,
A touch of warmth from the sun.

Radiance dances in the night,
Illuminating pure delight.
In the silence, we find peace,
As night's whispers slowly cease.

With every star that starts to fade,
In the shadows, dreams are laid.
In this still, divine embrace,
We find our solace, our place.

Celestial Ice Sculptures

Glistening formations in the night,
Whispers of wonder in silver light.
Frozen shapes from dreams untold,
Carved by stars, a sight to behold.

Crystals dance with the winter breeze,
Nature's art, it aims to please.
Each icy figure tells a tale,
Of winter nights in a hush so frail.

Glows of blue and hints of white,
Shimmering softly, pure delight.
A gallery hung in the air,
Celestial wonders beyond compare.

With every breath, they start to fade,
Moments cherished, vividly made.
Yet in the stillness, magic stays,
In frozen wonders, night displays.

So pause and gaze at this night sky,
Where fleeting beauty does not die.
Ice sculptures in the moonlit glow,
Celestial dreams in the soft, white snow.

The Sparkle of Stillness

In the quiet of the morning air,
Sunlight glimmers with gentle care.
Each droplet hangs on blades of grass,
Nature's gems, like crystals, pass.

Whispers of silence, soft and clear,
Echoes of calm, so pure and near.
The world awakes from slumber deep,
In this moment, peace we keep.

Shadows retreat as light appears,
Washing away the night's dark fears.
Every sparkle, a song unsung,
A tapestry of life, once spun.

Breath held close in this tranquil space,
Time slows down; we find our place.
Nature's beauty, a timeless thrill,
The sparkle of stillness, hearts to fill.

So let us linger, savor the still,
In this bright moment, as we will.
The day unfolds with gentle grace,
Where the sparkle of stillness we embrace.

Frost's Artful Touch

Delicate patterns on windowpanes,
Nature's brush creates fine veins.
Frosty whispers weave and swirl,
Magic dances, a hidden girl.

Every breath becomes a plume,
In winter's grip, the world finds bloom.
Shapes that glisten, twinkle, and spin,
An artful touch, where dreams begin.

Crystalline flowers, silent cheer,
In their presence, we draw near.
Captivated by nature's craft,
Frost's touch leaves us all daft.

Leave the warmth, embrace the cold,
Frosted stories yet untold.
In the quiet, magic thrums,
As winter's heartbeat softly hums.

So let us wander and take delight,
In winter's canvas, pure and bright.
Frost's artful touch, so soft and clear,
A fleeting masterpiece we hold dear.

Icy Lullabies

Whispers of winter, soft and low,
Gentle lullabies that ebb and flow.
Moonlight drapes on a frosty scene,
Dreams take flight on wings of sheen.

Stars hum sweetly, night sings along,
Every flake joins in the song.
Nature cradles the world in white,
Icy lullabies of pure delight.

The wind carries tales from afar,
Each note a wish on a drifting star.
Wrapped in warmth, we drift away,
In the embrace of frosty play.

Listen closely; hear the sound,
Of winter's magic, all around.
Icy breezes, soft and light,
Cradle us through the quiet night.

As slumber whispers, peace does reign,
In dreams of snow, we find our gain.
Icy lullabies softly sway,
Guiding us through night and day.

Glistening Silence

In the stillness of the night,
Whispers spread like silver light.
Stars above twinkle and gleam,
Embracing shadows in a dream.

Moon hangs low, a watchful gaze,
Guiding thoughts through softest haze.
Footsteps hush on frosted ground,
Nature's peace is gently found.

Crickets sing their lullabies,
Beneath the vast and starlit skies.
Each breath is crisp, a fleeting sound,
In the magic, we are bound.

Snowflakes fall, a gentle kiss,
Wrapping the world in tranquil bliss.
Every flake a tale to tell,
In this glistening silence, we dwell.

Whispers dance on frosty air,
Nature's secrets, soft and rare.
In this moment, hearts align,
Lost in the glistening silence, divine.

The Icy Veil

A breath of chill upon the skin,
Winter's touch, a quiet begin.
Branches draped in crystal lace,
Whispers of an icy grace.

Frosty windows, patterns spun,
Capturing the morning sun.
Every edge a diamond's hue,
Nature's art, forever new.

Footprints lead where shadows fade,
Through a world that dreams are made.
Every step a story told,
In the air, a secret cold.

Frozen rivers, silent flow,
Beneath the surface, life can grow.
Nature rests under the ice,
Waiting for the sun's warm slice.

Behind the veil, a life unseen,
Everything waits, poised and keen.
With every thaw, the truth revealed,
In the whispers of the icy field.

Frosted Elegance

Dew drops cling to emerald leaves,
A touch of frost, the heart believes.
In the garden, silence reigns,
Beauty found in whispered pains.

Petals kissed by winter's breath,
In this stillness, life and death.
Each bloom cloaked in icy sheen,
Nature's canvas, pure and clean.

The sparkle glows in dawn's embrace,
Highlighting every hidden place.
Frosted elegance unfolds,
In the sunlight, magic holds.

Every flake, a piece of art,
Painting dreams within the heart.
Fragrant memories linger long,
In this landscape, we belong.

Frosted branches touch the sky,
Whispers of winter passing by.
In the silence, secrets dance,
In the beauty, take a chance.

Celestial Frigid Dreams

Underneath this starry dome,
I drift in a celestial home.
Frigid winds and silver streams,
Carry softly whispered dreams.

Glacial light, a haunting glow,
Illuminates the paths we know.
In the night, the world remains,
Cradled in soft, frozen chains.

Snowflakes fall like shooting stars,
Bringing wishes from afar.
Each one holds a hope so dear,
In the hush, I feel you near.

Frigid breath on winter's cheek,
In this silence, words are weak.
Yet in dreams, we come alive,
In a dance, we learn to thrive.

Celestial realms, so pure and bright,
Guide us deeper through the night.
In this frost, we find our way,
Through celestial dreams, we sway.

Glacial Whispers

In the silence of the night,
Whispers dance on icy air,
Gentle echoes of the past,
Cold secrets everywhere.

Moonlight weaves its silver thread,
Crystals shimmer on the ground,
Nature's voice, a breath so light,
In stillness, magic found.

Frost-kissed trees in shadows stir,
Branches cradle puffs of snow,
Every twig a story holds,
Ancient tales from long ago.

Beneath a star-streaked velvet sky,
Glacial rivers softly flow,
Carving paths through time and dreams,
In their depths, the cold winds blow.

Listen closely to the night,
For the whispers never cease,
In the glacial breath of time,
Find a moment's quiet peace.

Luminescent Frost

In the dawn's first light, it shines,
Frost aglow on fields of white,
Each blade of grass, a diamond sky,
Nature's canvas, pure delight.

Winds hum softly through the trees,
Glittering gems on branches sway,
Every shadow holds a glow,
Painting dreams in frozen spray.

A crystal veil upon the lake,
Mirrors whisper of the storm,
While the sun begins to break,
Radiance hiding in its form.

Footsteps crunch on winter's breath,
Every sound a fleeting note,
In the stillness, life unfolds,
With each ripple, dreams afloat.

As twilight wraps the world in grace,
Luminescent frost appears,
A quiet end to day's embrace,
Whispers echo through the years.

Luminous Chill

As twilight descends, the hush grows,
A luminous chill fills the air,
Stars ignite as night unfolds,
Whispers of winter, soft and rare.

Silvery mists curl around the pines,
Breath of frost on every breath,
Nature's silence speaks so clear,
In this moment, life and death.

Underneath the moon's pale gaze,
Ice-bound dreams begin to flow,
Every sigh, a tale untold,
In the glow, our spirits grow.

Chilled fingers trace the frost-kissed glass,
A tapestry of shimmered light,
In this realm where hearts can feel,
Time suspends, sorrow takes flight.

Embraced by night, we find our peace,
In luminous chill, we sway and glide,
Through the stillness, our worries cease,
In winter's heart, we bide.

A Glint in the Frost

Before the dawn, a glint appears,
Frosty whispers on the ground,
Nature hides her secrets well,
In every sparkle, dreams abound.

A carpet laid of icy lace,
Every step, a crunching sound,
Life held close in frigid arms,
In the beauty lost, we're found.

Gentle touches from the skies,
Signatures left on branches bare,
Each crystal shard tells a story,
Of warm hearts beneath the care.

With every breath, the chill ignites,
A flicker of warmth in bitter cold,
In this world of silvered light,
We find the courage to be bold.

Among the frost and whispering trees,
A glint of hope begins to rise,
In the quiet, we find our strength,
As morning breaks, a world of ties.

Frosted Whispers

In the silence of the night,
Soft flakes tumble, a feather's flight.
Whispers of frost on the ancient trees,
Nature's breath in the gentle breeze.

Moonlight dances on icy ground,
A shimmering hush, no other sound.
Stars twinkle like diamonds in the sky,
Beneath their gaze, all dreams may fly.

Footsteps muffled in frosty air,
A world transformed, beyond compare.
Branches adorned in lacey white,
Embracing the magic of tranquil night.

Each flake tells a tale from above,
Of winter's grip, of peace and love.
A symphony played with delicate grace,
In this frosted land, we find our place.

Sparkling wonder, a breathless spell,
Caught in the stories we yearn to tell.
As morning breaks with golden rays,
Frosted whispers greet our days.

Glacial Reverie

Silent paths through frozen dreams,
Where time flows slow in silver streams.
Crystalline dawns, a radiant sight,
Awakening whispers in morning light.

Mountains stand with their icy crowns,
Guardians of echoes, nature's sounds.
A world encased in glassy hue,
Where everything feels fresh and new.

Snowflakes waltz in the pastel sky,
Choreographed by the winds' soft sigh.
In this glacial realm, dreams take flight,
Carried far by the wings of night.

Mirrored lakes reflecting the sky,
In their depths, secrets lie.
Each ripple brings forth a hidden tale,
Of glacial whispers on winter's trail.

Silent nights hold a quiet grace,
In this reverie, we find our place.
Beneath the stars, a gentle balm,
In the heart of winter, peace is calm.

Crystal Dreams

In the stillness of twilight's glow,
Crystal dreams begin to flow.
A tapestry woven with moonlit threads,
Whispers of magic where wonder spreads.

Glistening paths lead hearts away,
Where shadows dance and fairies play.
Each step taken on the frozen ground,
Echoes of beauty in silence found.

Icicles hang like daggers bright,
Catching the spark of the fading light.
Nature's jewels, pure and rare,
Crafting a canvas beyond compare.

As night descends in deep embrace,
We dream of hope in this sacred space.
With every breath, a wish we send,
In crystal dreams, our hearts transcend.

Night softens into a tranquil haze,
As the world rests, lost in a daze.
Wrapped in wonder, we gently sigh,
In crystal dreams, we learn to fly.

Echoes of Winter Light

Through the forest, whispers weave,
Echoes of light that we believe.
Frost-kissed branches, a silvery glow,
Guiding us gently through layers of snow.

Glimmers of warmth in the frosty air,
A dance of shadows, pure and rare.
Each ray of sunlight, a fleeting kiss,
Crafting moments that we can't miss.

In the heart of winter, stillness reigns,
Nature's lullaby, a sweet refrain.
Every flake falls with purpose clear,
Whispering secrets for us to hear.

As light plays tricks in the evening sky,
Colors shimmer and softly sigh.
Echoes of joy in every flurry,
In winter's embrace, there's no worry.

With every breath, a tale unfolds,
In the glow of winter, our spirit holds.
In echoes of light, we find our way,
Guided by dreams that never sway.

The Cold Embrace

In silence falls the snow,
A blanket soft and white,
Where whispers of the wind go,
And day turns into night.

The trees stand still and bare,
Adorned with crystal lace,
Each branch has tales to share,
In winter's chill embrace.

Footprints in the frosted ground,
A story left behind,
In every step, a sound,
Of seasons intertwined.

A world transformed anew,
With shadows played in light,
The cold wraps me like dew,
In dreams of frozen sight.

In this serene retreat,
I find a tranquil space,
Where every heartbeat's beat,
Is held in cold embrace.

Winter's Twinkle

Stars above, they glimmer bright,
In the still of the night sky,
Each flake that dances, pure delight,
A fleeting wish, a gentle sigh.

The moon's glow casts a silver hue,
On crystals glinting on the ground,
In quiet moments, dreams come true,
Where magic swirls all around.

Frosted edges, nature's art,
On windowpanes, a delicate trace,
Each pattern plays a vital part,
In winter's waltz, an elegant grace.

The chill wraps tight, but hearts feel warm,
In the glow of twilight's kiss,
As laughter breaks the winter's charm,
An echo of nostalgic bliss.

As dawn arrives, the sky ignites,
A canvas painted gold and blue,
Bringing forth the day's delights,
In winter's twinkle, dreams renew.

Glacial Artistry

A frozen lake, so clear and bright,
Like glass beneath the azure sky,
Reflections twirling in the light,
Where whispers of the cold winds sigh.

Icicles hanging, sharp and proud,
Nature's daggers, glimmering sheen,
A silent beauty, tranquil crowd,
In icy realms, a painter's dream.

Beneath the snow, life hides away,
A secret world of dreams untold,
In silent shrouds, they gently sway,
Where frozen tales will soon unfold.

The mountains stand, a fortress grand,
Crowned in white, they touch the clouds,
Majestic strength that time has planned,
In winter's veil, they wear their shrouds.

As night descends, the stars peek through,
A symphony of ice and light,
In this vast realm, I feel anew,
Glacial artistry, pure delight.

Choreography of Ice

In the quiet of the frost,
Life dances in the crystal air,
Nature's artistry embossed,
A delicate ballet laid bare.

The whirlwinds spin, a frosty caste,
Snowflakes twirl in swirling grace,
In winter's grip, a spell is cast,
As beauty holds a gentle pace.

Branches sway with elegant poise,
A symphony of silence plays,
Each note a whisper, soft, no noise,
In this serene and frozen maze.

The river flows, then slows to freeze,
A mirror holding winter's face,
In frozen form, it aims to please,
A tranquil, mesmerizing trace.

In moments lost, I feel the time,
Where every breath a soft caress,
In nature's dance, so pure, sublime,
The choreography of ice, no less.

Frosted Pearls

In dawn's soft light, they gleam,
Frosted treasures, nature's dream.
A silent beauty, pure and bright,
Whispers softly through the night.

Each blade of grass, a jeweled dance,
Reflecting moments, life's romance.
A world encrusted, fresh and new,
In winter's grasp, a stunning view.

The chill embraces every flake,
A quilt of white, serene, awake.
With every breath, a chilled delight,
As day unfolds, the frost takes flight.

In glistening fields, serenity,
Nature's bounty, wild and free.
With every step, a crackling sound,
In frosted pearls, true peace is found.

So let us wander, hand in hand,
Through sparkling lands, so softly planned.
Amidst the pearls, beneath the sky,
In frosted wonders, we will fly.

Glittering Solitude

Amidst the trees, a quiet hush,
Where shadows fade and breezes rush.
Each glimmer caught in branches high,
A sense of peace that will not die.

Beneath the stars, a gentle glow,
In solitude, the heart will flow.
The world outside, a distant sound,
In glittering stillness, dreams abound.

The moonlight dances on the snow,
Like whispered secrets, soft and slow.
With every breath, a world serene,
In shimmering calm, the heart's unseen.

A moment captured, pure and bright,
In glittering solitude, the night.
Each flake that falls, a whispered prayer,
In quietude, we find our share.

Embrace the stillness, lost in thought,
In this calm space, our souls are caught.
With every spark, a memory made,
In glittering solitude, unafraid.

Icebound Wonders

Frozen streams, a still cascade,
Magic woven, nature's jade.
In icy realms where dreams reside,
Icebound wonders, love and pride.

The frost inscribes on every leaf,
Stories old, both joy and grief.
A crystal world, both sharp and pure,
In winter's breath, we found our cure.

Each flake a tale of days gone by,
Whispers lost among the sky.
With every shimmer, memories flare,
In icebound wonders, moments rare.

The earth adorned in silvery lace,
A canvas blank, a new embrace.
In chilly air, our laughter rings,
Among the magic, love still clings.

So let us wander through this maze,
In icebound wonders, lost in gaze.
With frozen dreams that softly fade,
In nature's grasp, our hearts are laid.

Enchantment in the Chill

In winter's grasp, the world enchants,
With every breath, the spirit dances.
The silence sings, a soothing thrill,
In every heart, there's magic still.

Snowflakes twirl like whispered dreams,
A gentle touch, or so it seems.
Through frost-kissed woods, we weave our way,
In enchantment found, we choose to stay.

The air is crisp, the night is young,
In frosted breath, our hearts are sung.
With every glimmer, every glance,
We find the joy in winter's prance.

The stars above, like diamonds bright,
In velvet skies, a wondrous sight.
Together, lost in this still spell,
In enchantment's arms, we gently dwell.

So hold my hand, and let us roam,
In winter's chill, we make our home.
With every heartbeat, warmth we fill,
In love's enchantment, time stands still.

Translucent Enchantment

In twilight's dance, shadows weave,
A whisper soft, the night deceives.
Moonlight spills on silver streams,
Hidden magic fuels our dreams.

Beneath the stars, a secret sigh,
Each twinkle holds a lullaby.
Branches whisper in the breeze,
Holding tales of ancient trees.

Colors blend in twilight's art,
A canvas painted from the heart.
Moments linger, softly spun,
Translucent dreams, we come undone.

Through veils of dusk, we wander slow,
A tapestry of ebb and flow.
In every breath the silence speaks,
Of gentle paths and hidden peaks.

Together we embrace the night,
In this embrace of pure delight.
With every spark, the world ignites,
Translucent hopes, endless heights.

The Luster of Winter's Breath

A crisp embrace, the frost awakes,
The world adorned in icy flakes.
Each breath released, like whispers fleet,
A tapestry of cold retreat.

Silver branches gleam in light,
Nature's diamond, pure and bright.
The earth lies still, a hushed refrain,
Wrapped in dreams of crystal gain.

Beneath the moon, a gentle glow,
Guides us through the path of snow.
Stars above, like scattered seeds,
Sow the warmth that winter breeds.

In the stillness, secrets swell,
A magic woven, hard to tell.
The heart beats fast, beneath the chill,
Winter's breath, a luring thrill.

With every step, the world enchants,
In nature's song, the spirit dances.
The luster found in every gleam,
Whispers softly of our dreams.

Frosted Luminescence

Beneath the frost, a glow unfolds,
A silent story, softly told.
Icicles hang like crystal fair,
Glistening dreams that fill the air.

Winter's breath, a chilling grace,
Embraces all in its gentle space.
Soft whispers glide on frozen streams,
Awakening the heart of dreams.

As night descends with starry eyes,
The frosted glow begins to rise.
A symphony of light and shade,
In icy realms, our hopes are laid.

Every flake, a dancing spark,
Creating wonders in the dark.
The world transformed in silver hues,
A frosted realm, a tranquil muse.

Boundless beauty, crystal clear,
In winter's grasp, we hold what's dear.
Frosted luminescence glows,
A whispered magic that still flows.

Tapestry of Glacial Light

Woven threads of ice and glow,
A tapestry where cold winds blow.
Each strand a story, told with care,
In glacial light, a world laid bare.

Mountains rise, with wisdom vast,
Guarding secrets of the past.
Rivers dance through frozen halls,
Echoing nature's cooling calls.

As evening falls, the colors shift,
A glimmering haze, a silent gift.
Veils of light across the ground,
In every shadow, beauty found.

Gentle whispers in the night,
Illuminated, hearts take flight.
In the stillness, time unwinds,
With every breath, the glimmer binds.

Together, we embrace the chill,
In the tapestry, we find the thrill.
Glacial light, a dance so bright,
Guides us softly, through the night.

Frosty Luminescence

Beneath the silver moon's glow,
The frost whispers in the night,
Each flake a silent story,
Sparkling with pure delight.

Trees draped in icy splendor,
Glistening branches sway low,
Nature's delicate canvas,
Where magic begins to flow.

Fields blanketed in white,
Soft footprints tell of dreams,
In the stillness of the hour,
Life's mystery softly gleams.

Stars twinkle in the cold air,
Guiding the wanderer's way,
In a world wrapped in silence,
Waiting for break of day.

Frosty luminescence shines,
Illuminating the dark,
A reminder of beauty,
In the heart, it leaves a mark.

Echoes of Winter Light

Echoes dance in winter's breath,
A soft sigh across the land,
Shadows blend with pale light,
Caressed by a gentle hand.

Drifting snowflakes spin and twirl,
Each one unique in its flight,
Whispers of a season's song,
Chiming with pure delight.

Frozen streams reflect the sky,
Mirroring the heavens' hue,
A canvas of blue and white,
Winter's artistry shines through.

In the quiet, secrets dwell,
Crystals form with every breath,
Nature's peace, a sacred space,
Beyond the grip of death.

Echoes linger in the air,
Carried on the winter's chill,
A melody of silence,
In our hearts, it echoes still.

Gleaming in the Freeze

Gleaming in the frozen dawn,
The world is kissed by ice,
Sunlight dances on the ground,
Breaking through, oh so nice.

Every step on crunching snow,
Sings a song of crisp delight,
Moments held in purest form,
Twinkling in the soft light.

Clouds move slowly overhead,
Casting shadows over fields,
In this hush, a tale unfolds,
With every breath, it yields.

Icicles hang like diamonds,
Adorning roofs and trees,
Nature's art defies the cold,
To capture hearts with ease.

Gleaming in the winter's grasp,
The beauty takes its hold,
A reminder of the warmth,
In a world that's bright and bold.

Prismatic Crystals

Prismatic crystals form anew,
In the silent frosty air,
Each one reflects a spectrum,
A wondrous sight so rare.

Fractals dance in morning light,
Painting rainbows on the snow,
Nature's palette spills its hues,
In a graceful, flowing show.

The world feels alive with magic,
As shadows stretch and bend,
A tapestry of colors,
In the quiet, there's no end.

Beneath the frost, life waits still,
Holding dreams in frozen frames,
When warmth returns, they'll awaken,
Igniting passion's flames.

Prismatic crystals shimmer bright,
A dance of light and shade,
In winter's embrace, a reminder,
Of the art that nature made.

Serene Splendor

In the quiet dawn, light breaks,
Colors softly kiss the sky,
Nature breathes a gentle peace,
Awakening the world's sigh.

Mountains stand with grace and might,
Rivers dance with joyful flow,
Trees embrace the morning sun,
Whispering secrets, low and slow.

Fields of gold in sunlight shine,
Flowers nod with fragrant cheer,
Every petal tells a tale,
Serenity is drawing near.

Clouds drift by in soft embrace,
Time seems sweet in every glance,
Moments fade like fleeting dreams,
In splendor, we find our chance.

Let us linger, heart in hand,
In this tranquil, sacred space,
Serene splendor wraps us tight,
In harmony, we find our place.

The Gleam Between Seasons

Leaves transition with gentle grace,
Colors blend in perfect dance,
Whispers of the autumn breeze,
Invite the frost, a fleeting chance.

Sunlight weaves through branches bare,
Casting shadows, long and thin,
Yet a warmth still lingers here,
In the twilight's soft, dim grin.

Winter's breath is drawing near,
But hope clings to every tree,
The gleam of light between the storms,
Reminds us of what used to be.

Nature pauses, time stands still,
In this realm of shifting shades,
Moments stretch, like dreams unsung,
A bridge where past and future fades.

Let us cherish this brief glow,
Where seasons meet and gently sway,
In the gleam between the times,
Life reveals its tender play.

Shards of Frost

Morning breaks with icy breath,
Shards of frost on window panes,
Nature wraps in crystal lace,
Every glance, a cold refrain.

Fields lie still beneath the chill,
Silence echoes in the dawn,
A frozen world, so pure, so bright,
Yet within, the heart goes on.

Sunlight pierces through the haze,
Transforming frost to silver light,
Moments glisten, time stands still,
In this beauty, pure delight.

Yet shadows linger, whispers call,
Of warmth that waits beneath the cold,
Shards of frost, like fleeting dreams,
In their grasp, a story told.

Let us walk through winter's gaze,
Feel the magic in the air,
For even in the sharpest chill,
Love's warmth is always there.

Whispering Fragments of Cold

In the night, the stars do gleam,
Whispers soft, like winter's breath,
Fragments of a world undone,
In the silence, echoes left.

Snowflakes dance on gentle winds,
Each one tells a tale alone,
Bringing magic to the hush,
Of a season carved in stone.

Branches bare, a silhouette,
Against the moon's soft, silver glow,
Night reveals its hidden thoughts,
In the chill, truth starts to flow.

Every shadow hints at dreams,
Lost in whispers, gentle, deep,
Fragments of the cold embrace,
Cradle secrets as we sleep.

So let the quiet fill your heart,
With every breath, the night unfold,
In the realm of winter's grace,
Discover warmth in whispers cold.

9 789916 799000